Our New Car

Ratios and Proportions

Nola Quinlan

Consultants

Pamela Dase, M.A.Ed.
National Board Certified Teacher

Barbara Talley, M.S.
Texas A&M University

Publishing Credits

Dona Herweck Rice, *Editor-in-Chief*
Robin Erickson, *Production Director*
Lee Aucoin, *Creative Director*
Timothy J. Bradley, *Illustration Manager*
Sara Johnson, M.S.Ed., *Senior Editor*
Aubrie Nielsen, M.S.Ed., *Associate Education Editor*
Jennifer Kim, M.A.Ed., *Associate Education Editor*
Neri Garcia, *Senior Designer*
Stephanie Reid, *Photo Editor*
Rachelle Cracchiolo, M.S.Ed., *Publisher*

Image Credits

Cover egd/Shutterstock, (inset) Relja/Shutterstock; p.1 egd/Shutterstock, (inset) Relja/Shutterstock; p.3 Pincasso/Shutterstock; p.4 Barry Austin Photography/Getty Images; p.4–5 Laitr Keiows/Shutterstock; p.5 (top) Max Earey/Shutterstock, (bottom) Laitr Keiows/Shutterstock; p.6 (left) Charlie Hutton/Shutterstock, (right) L Barnwell/Shutterstock, (top) jamalludin/Shutterstock; p.6–7 Studio 37/Shutterstock; p.8 Henry Hazboun/Shutterstock; p.8–9 egd/Shutterstock; p.9 (left) Gary Paul Lewis/Shutterstock, (right) Gunter Nezhoda/Shutterstock; p.10 Centurion Studio/Shutterstock; p.10–11 ROBERTO ZILLI/Shutterstock; p.12 (top) Barry Austin Photography/Getty Images, (bottom) Uppercut/Getty Images; p.12–13 Andrr/Shutterstock; p.14 (top) Valua Vitaly/Shutterstock, (bottom) Susan Mackenzie/Shutterstock; p.14–15 Stefan Ataman/Shutterstock; p.15 (top) michaeljung/Shutterstock, (bottom) Vereshchagin Dmitry/Shutterstock; p.16 (top) pistolseven/Shutterstock, (bottom) Laitr Keiows/Shutterstock; p.16–17 Mikhail/Shutterstock; p.17 Stefan Ataman/Shutterstock; p.18 gary718/Shutterstock; p.18–19 Maxim Blinkov/Shutterstock; p.19 Juan Camilo Bernal/Shutterstock, (inset) D&D Photos/Shutterstock; p.20 Selena/Shutterstock; p.20-21 visuelldesign/Shutterstock; p.21 Christoff/Shutterstock; p.22 (left) thelatin10/BigStock, (right) Barry Austin Photography/Getty Images; p.22–23 Carroteater/Dreamstime; p.24 (left) Amy Walters/Shutterstock, (right) cjp/iStockphoto; p.24–25 Zeljko Radojko/Shutterstock; p.25 lightpoet/Shutterstock; p.26 Barry Austin Photography/Getty Images; p.26–27 Alexander Chaikin/Shutterstock; p.27 Barry Austin Photography/Getty Images; p.28 WendellandCarolyn/iStockphoto

Teacher Created Materials

5301 Oceanus Drive
Huntington Beach, CA 92649-1030
http://www.tcmpub.com

ISBN 978-1-4333-3451-1

© 2012 Teacher Created Materials, Inc.

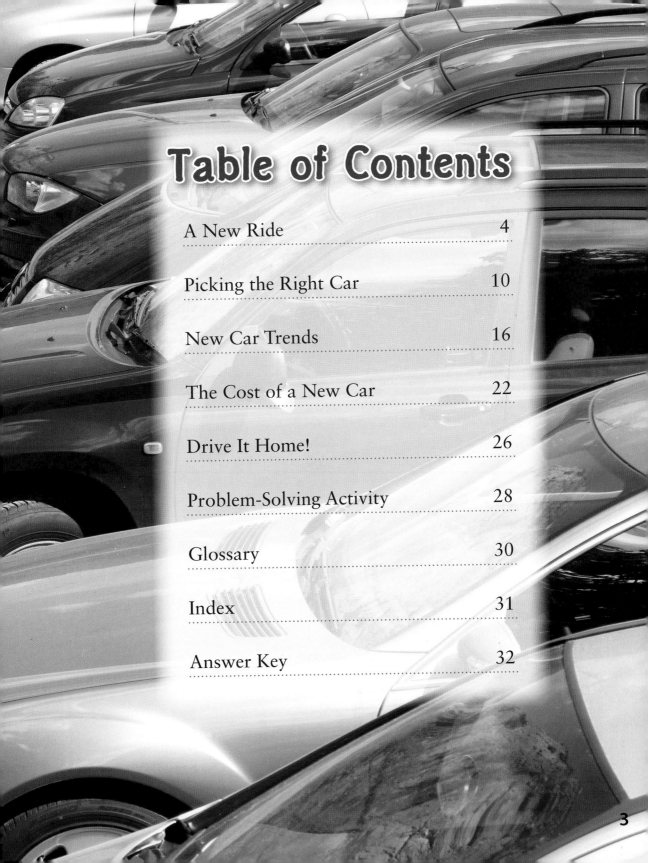

Table of Contents

A New Ride

I'm so excited! Today my parents are picking me up from school in our new car. We all feel very lucky to have our new car. It has been a long time since we bought a car, and we really needed it. Our old car broke down way too often. My parents wanted a car that would be more reliable and safer for our family.

Buying a car was fun, but it was also a lot of work. I had no idea how many choices we would have to make. My dad said that he was really glad we did our homework before we made our purchase!

Auto Shows

Some people go to auto shows to check out the latest **innovations** (in-uh-VEY-shuhnz) in cars. Many carmakers unveil their latest designs at an auto show.

FORCE DE L'EFFICIENCE: HIGH PRECISION INJECTION.

Did You Know?

Over 50 million new cars are produced each year worldwide. China produces the most cars, followed by Japan and the United States.

What Is a Ratio?

A **ratio** (REY-shee-oh) compares two quantities. For example, if a car lot had 12 minivans and 15 compact cars, the ratio of minivans to compact cars could be expressed as 12 to 15, 12:15, or $\frac{12}{15}$. The ratio of compact cars to minivans could be expressed as 15 to 12, 15:12, or $\frac{15}{12}$.

I always thought that when you needed a new car, you walked into a car dealership and picked one out. My parents taught me that it is better to do some research before making a final decision. A car costs a lot of money! People should take their time and learn as much as they can before they spend a large amount of money on any item, including a car.

The first thing to decide when looking for a new car is what kind of car you want to buy. People choose cars for different reasons. Some people want a safe car. Others want one with room for kids or cargo. Some drivers are more interested in how fast a car goes or how it handles on the highway. It is important to know statistics about the manufacturer (man-yuh-FAK-cher-er) as well as the model and make of the car you are interested in, so you can make an informed decision.

Equivalent Ratios

Ratios can be simplified just like fractions. The ratio 12:15 can be simplified to the ratio 4:5 by dividing each part by 3. The ratios 12:15 and 4:5 are called **equivalent ratios**.

LET'S EXPLORE MATH

When automobile dealers order cars, they consider the most popular colors. The manager of Metropolitan Automobiles asked his son, Ian, to count the number of red cars and black cars that travel past the dealership on a Saturday morning. He asked his daughter, Lola, to count white cars. Ian counted 75 red cars and 50 black cars. Lola counted 60 white cars.

a. Express the following ratios in simplest form:

- red to black cars
- black to white cars
- red to white cars

b. How many cars did Ian and Lola count all together?

c. Express the following ratios in simplest form:

- red cars to total cars
- total cars to black cars

d. Is the ratio of red to black the same as the ratio of black to red? How are they related?

e. Why is it necessary to express a ratio in words?

There are many choices to make when you buy a car. My parents discussed whether to buy a new car or a used car. They also considered leasing a car instead of buying one. Leasing a car is like renting an apartment. You make monthly payments to use the car, but you will not own it at the end of the leasing period.

A used car is a car that was previously owned by another driver. That means it has already been driven and used for some period of time. Used cars are usually less expensive than new cars. That reason alone is why many drivers are interested in them. When you buy a used car, you need to make sure it is in good condition. Cars that have been driven for many miles may need extra **maintenance** (MEYN-tuh-nuhns). If a used car needs to be fixed often, it may not cost less after all.

New cars come directly from the factory. They are sold by car dealers. Most dealers have lots of different makes, models, colors, and features in the cars on their lot. You have a good chance of finding exactly what you want. Also, manufacturers of cars offer a **warranty** (WAWR-uhn-tee) on a new car. If you have any problems with the car while it is still fairly new, you can take it to a dealer for repairs. With the warranty, the repairs will be free!

Picking the Right Car

People are passionate about their cars. Drivers compare many different makes and models when they are shopping for a car. Some customers are loyal to a certain brand. My mom was not loyal to a car brand. She wanted to shop around.

Other drivers are attracted to new, cutting-edge car models. It can be risky to buy a new model that has not been tested for very long. But if they perform well, they may become quite popular.

Color is very important to many car shoppers. My parents discussed color a lot! Customers usually have a color in mind when they begin their search.

One car dealership we visited had 3 SUVs for every 5 sedans. This means that for every 12 SUVs, there were 20 sedans. A **proportion** is formed by two equal ratios. $\frac{3}{5} = \frac{12}{20}$ is an example of a proportion. It says that the ratio of 3 to 5 is the same as the ratio of 12 to 20. You can think about this proportion just like fractions. To make a proportion, you must multiply the first and second terms by the same number, which is the same as multiplying by 1.

$$\frac{3}{5} \cdot \frac{4}{4} = \frac{12}{20}$$

Writing Proportions

When you write a proportion, it is important that the two ratios describe the items in the same order. Suppose you know that there are red and black cars at a car dealership and the ratio of red cars to black cars is 5:8. If you know that there are 50 red cars at the dealership, you can find the number of black cars by writing the proportion $\frac{5}{8} = \frac{50}{y}$. Notice that the number that represents red cars is on the top of each ratio and the number for black cars is on the bottom. In order to get from 5 to 50, you multiply by 10. To keep the ratios proportional, you multiply 8 by 10 as well.

$$\frac{5}{8} \cdot \frac{10}{10} = \frac{50}{80}$$

There would be 80 black cars.

LET'S EXPLORE MATH

At one dealership we visited, I decided to count black and white cars on the lot while my parents talked with the salesperson. I counted 25 white cars and 40 black cars.

a. Give the following ratios of the cars in simplest form: white to black, black to white, white to total cars, and black to total cars.

I also counted black and white cars at two other dealerships. The ratio of white to black cars was the same as the ratio at the first dealership.

b. I counted 160 black cars at the second dealership. Write a proportion that could be used to find the number of white cars. How many white cars are there at the second dealership?

c. I counted a total of 195 cars at the third dealership. Write a proportion that could be used to find the number of black cars. How many black cars are there at the third dealership?

d. How many white cars are there at the third dealership? How did you find the number of white cars? How else could you have found the number of white cars?

11

There are still more choices after you have selected the make and color of your new car. The trick is to find the right car for you and your lifestyle. My parents considered a lot of options before we picked our car. They thought about whether we needed four-wheel drive. This feature is helpful for people who often drive in snow or ice. It allows all four wheels to be powered by the engine at the same time. Our family decided that feature was not important for us.

My mom's main concern was the size of the car. She carpools to work with several other people in our neighborhood. She wanted to make sure that we had a car with enough seat belts for all of her carpool members.

The two "end" numbers in a proportion are called *extremes*. The "middle" numbers are called the *means*.

means

$$3{:}5 = 12{:}20$$

extremes

Many people carpool to work to save money on gas, to help reduce pollution from cars, or to use the faster carpool lane on a highway.

Cross-Multiplication

Another way to find a missing quantity in a proportion is to use cross-multiplication. In every proportion, the product of the extremes is equal to the product of the means. Let's say you are asked to solve the following proportion for x: $\frac{3}{6} = \frac{x}{8}$

Using cross-multiplication, set the product of the means equal to the product of the extremes:

$$x \cdot 6 = 3 \cdot 8$$
$$6x = 24$$
$$\frac{6x}{6} = \frac{24}{6}$$
$$x = 4$$

If you draw a line from x to 6 and 3 to 8, you can see why this method is called *cross-multiplication*.

On a used-car lot, the ratio of blue cars to the total number of cars is 2:15.

a. Write a proportion and find out how many blue cars there are if there are 90 cars on the lot.

b. Write a proportion and find out how many cars are on the lot if there are 14 blue cars.

Safety is important to all car owners. It was very important to my mom and dad! Car owners want to know they will be protected if they are in an accident.

Cars now come equipped with many different safety features. My mom told me this was not always the case. Seat belts became **standard** in all cars in the late 1950s. Before that, people could choose whether they wanted seat belts in their cars. Seatbelts were invented to keep passengers inside their vehicle during an accident. They are the most effective way to prevent injury and death in a car accident.

Safe Braking

Many cars today have an anti-lock brake system. This system prevents the wheels from locking, which could cause a car to skid across the road. Some new models even have automatic braking. Cars with this technology can sense when another object is too close and can apply the brakes to avoid a collision—without the driver even touching the brake pedal!

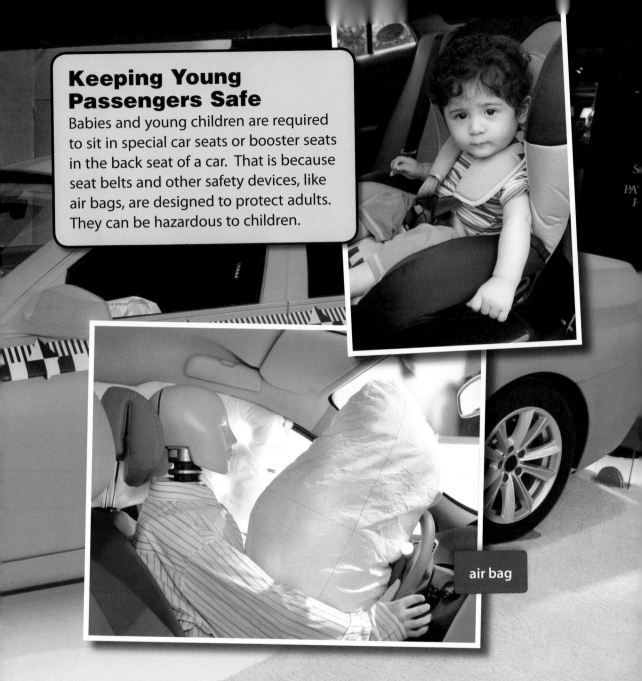

Keeping Young Passengers Safe

Babies and young children are required to sit in special car seats or booster seats in the back seat of a car. That is because seat belts and other safety devices, like air bags, are designed to protect adults. They can be hazardous to children.

air bag

Air bags are safety devices that became widely used in cars in the early 1990s. They are standard for the front seat area of cars. Air bags are hidden but are released and inflate quickly in the event of a collision. They protect passengers from hitting hard objects inside the car, like the steering wheel or a window.

A car designer sketches concepts.

New Car Trends

Every year, manufacturers produce new cars. Each year, the cars are more advanced than those of the year before. Engineers test concept cars and use what they learn to create new cars that consumers will be excited to drive. Every year, designers find new ways to make cars look fast and powerful.

Drivers consider the latest trends when they choose a car to buy. **Fuel efficiency** (ih-FISH-uhn-see) is a popular trend in cars today because gas is expensive. Many consumers pay close attention to the gas mileage of cars. This statistic tells a car owner how much gas the car needs to cover a certain distance. The more gasoline a car uses, the more it costs to drive. Using less gas is also a good way to protect our planet.

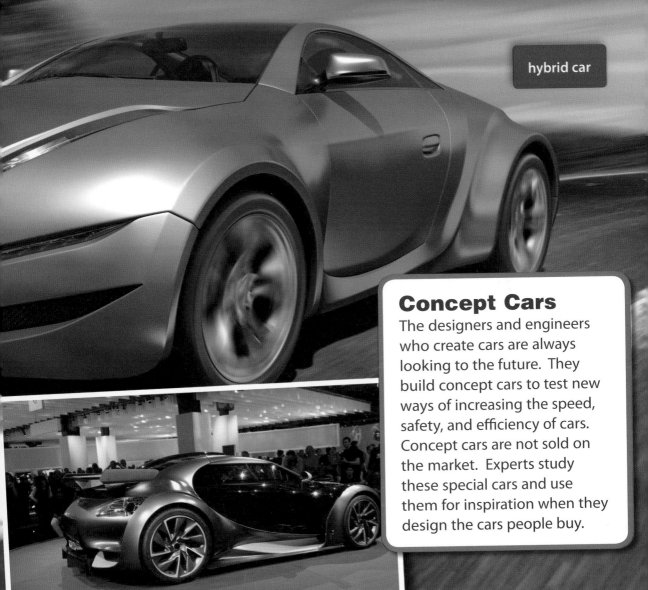

A hybrid (HAHY-brid) car is a popular choice for someone who wants the best gas mileage possible. Hybrids use two different power sources to move the car—usually a gas engine and an electric motor. This combination allows hybrids to be more efficient at using fuel for certain driving conditions. Manufacturers are also working on innovative cars that are powered by the sun's energy.

hybrid car

Concept Cars

The designers and engineers who create cars are always looking to the future. They build concept cars to test new ways of increasing the speed, safety, and efficiency of cars. Concept cars are not sold on the market. Experts study these special cars and use them for inspiration when they design the cars people buy.

Today, cars **emit** (ih-MIT) a lot of pollution into the air. Cars that burn less gas create less pollution. Manufacturers are working hard to create cars that can keep our air cleaner.

Many people believe that electric cars can help solve the problem of pollution caused by gas emissions. These cars have electric motors that provide their power. An electric car plugs into a special socket to be recharged. It is powered by electricity just like a computer or a refrigerator. Since you have electricity in your home, it is like having a gas station right in your carport or garage!

New Again

Have you ever seen an old car that looks different from every other car on the road? It might be bigger or it might not even have windows, but it is still bright and shiny. Car lovers get excited about antique (an-TEEK) cars that are still in beautiful condition. Car shows and clubs are devoted to honoring old cars from every decade.

An electric car plugs in to recharge.

Gas Mileage

Gas mileage is an example of a **rate**. It is the number of miles traveled per gallon (kilometers per liter) of gasoline burned. The gas mileage that your car gets will determine how often you will need to fill your tank. Some cars use gas quickly, while other models are more efficient at using fuel.

Car buyers that know a lot about how a car operates are often interested in how it feels when they drive it. These types of customers usually look under the hood and see what kind of engine is there. That can tell them a lot about how a car will perform. My parents were not interested in speed or engines. They just wanted a car that would take them where they need to go.

Ways to Measure Speed

The speed that a car travels is another example of a rate. The speed of a car is usually described in miles or kilometers per hour. That means the average number of miles or kilometers traveled in one hour.

However, speed could be described in other ways—feet per minute, miles per minute, inches per second, or meters per day. Basically, you can describe speed with any measure of distance per any measure of time.

The Bugatti Veyron is one of the world's fastest cars. It can travel up to 253 miles (407 km) per hour!

You can use a proportion to convert one rate of speed to another. To change 65 miles per hour to feet per hour, for example, multiply one rate by another.

Write 65 miles per hour as the fraction $\frac{65 \text{ miles}}{1 \text{ hour}}$. Write the conversion (5,280 feet per mile) as a fraction. Make sure the same unit of measure is the numerator in one fraction and the denominator in the other.

$$\frac{65 \text{ miles}}{1 \text{ hour}} \cdot \frac{5{,}280 \text{ feet}}{1 \text{ mile}} = 343{,}200 \text{ feet per hour}$$

When you divide 65 miles by 1 mile, the answer is 65. The unit of measure "cancels," leaving just a number. The answer to the conversion is in feet per hour, since those are the only units of measure left in the problem.

LET'S EXPLORE MATH

a. A car is traveling 30 mph. What is its speed in miles per day? (*Hint:* Think of how many hours are in a day.)

b. A runner is moving 720 feet per minute. What is the speed in mph? Round to the nearest mph. (*Hint:* Think of how many minutes are in an hour and how many feet are in a mile.)

The Cost of a New Car

Once my parents thought through all their choices, it was finally time to go to the dealership to make our purchase. We knew the make and model we wanted, and we had agreed on a color and what accessories were important. I was shocked at how long it took to actually buy the car. It certainly is not as easy as going into the store to buy a new pair of shoes!

Negotiating (ni-GOH-shee-eyt-ing) is an important part of buying a car. The customer can suggest a cost and see if the dealer will accept that offer. If not, there might have to be some **bargaining**. There are many different fees and charges, and you have to pay close attention to what they are. It can be very stressful. My parents did not really enjoy that part of their car-buying experience.

The car salesman offered my parents a **chrome** (KROHM) trim package at a discount of 20% with the purchase of any new car. The regular price of the package is $180. I determined the discount by solving the proportion: $\frac{n}{180} = \frac{20}{100}$.

The discount is $36, so the chrome trim package would cost us $144. Remember that if you take 20% off, 80% remains. You could have solved this problem by finding 80% of $180.

Percentages

A **percent** is a special kind of ratio. It is the ratio of a number to 100. For example, 20% means 20:100 or $\frac{20}{100}$. To solve any percent problem, rewrite it in the form: _____ is _____% of _____. Write a proportion to answer the question *What is 20% of $180?*

$$\frac{\$36}{\$180} = \frac{20}{100}$$

LET'S EXPLORE MATH

Write proportions to solve the problems below.

a. If Mrs. Davis paid $150 for her chrome trim package with a 20% discount, what was the original price of the package?

b. Mr. Hernandez bargained for a better discount on his chrome trim package. It originally cost $200 and he paid $155. What percent discount did he receive?

Any extra feature you want in a car may increase the final price. My parents had to decide which special features were really the most important for our family.

We knew we had to have air conditioning because it is so hot in the summer. We knew we did not need a sunroof. Those were easy choices. It was harder to decide if we should get a built-in **global positioning system (GPS)** device. That could come in handy if we are lost or on the road in a new place. Ultimately, my dad decided it was not worth the extra money. There were other features that my parents considered. They had to talk about all of them and make decisions to help them stay within their **budget**.

GPS

A/C

sunroof

LET'S EXPLORE MATH

Mr. McGregor is shopping for a new car. Solve the following problems by first writing a proportion and then solving for the missing number.

a. Mr. McGregor spends $20 to put 10 liters of gasoline in the car he has now. For one car they are interested in, he is told that it has a gas tank that holds 17 liters of gas. How much will it cost for a full tank of gas for that car? (*Hint:* Assume that the cost of gas per liter stays the same.)

b. Mr. McGregor will get a discount on his auto insurance if he gets a car with a built-in GPS device. The ratio of his annual auto insurance cost with a GPS device to his cost without a GPS device is 8:9. If the cost of insurance without a GPS is $630 a year, what will the cost be if he buys a car with a GPS device?

c. At one dealership, two of the cars inside the showroom do not have a sunroof, but the other three cars do. The proportion of cars with sunroofs in the outdoor lot is the same as the proportion inside the showroom. If 250 of the cars outside do not have sunroofs, how many cars in the outdoor lot have sunroofs?

Drive It Home!

After all that research and all those decisions, we finally bought a car! My family agrees it is the perfect car for us. My mom loves how big it is. A lot of kids will fit inside it. My dad is happy that the car has such high safety ratings. He also appreciates that it was affordable. I am excited that it has a good sound system for our music. All of us are very happy with the purchase.

There is no doubt that car shopping can be an overwhelming experience. There are many choices to make and so much to consider. The research you do is important. It will help you make a more educated choice. In the end, if you have done your homework, you will have "wheels" you can be proud of!

Midtown Auto Sales

Mrs. Lee, owner of Midtown Auto Sales, looked at the last two years of sales at her car dealership. She noticed an increase in hybrid car sales and would like to increase the amount of hybrids she has on the car lot. In order to do that, she must first decrease the amount of other types of cars that the dealership has in stock. Use the table below to answer the questions. Simplify your answers. Round percents to the nearest whole percent.

Midtown Auto Sales History 2011–2012

Car Type	2011 Sales	2012 Sales
sedan	320	285
sports car	103	72
truck	145	100
SUV	210	141
hybrid	90	156

Solve It!

a. What is the ratio of sales of hybrids to total cars in 2011? In 2012?

b. What percentage of sales was hybrids in 2011? In 2012?

c. What car type would you recommend Mrs. Lee decrease based on the 2011–2012 sales history?

d. Suppose Mrs. Lee's hybrid sales increased to 168 hybrids in 2013, and that total sales of cars increased in the same proportion from 2012 to 2013. How many cars would she have sold in 2013?

Use the steps below to help you answer the questions.

Step 1: Add the sales of all cars in 2011 and put that number under the number of hybrid cars. Simplify your answer by dividing both numbers by the same number. Repeat for 2012 sales.

Step 2: Write a sentence in the form _____ is _____ % of _____. Use a proportion to solve the problem.

Step 3: Think about which car types had low percentages of sales from 2011–2012. Calculate the percentages to verify your answer.

Step 4: Write a proportion to solve the problem. Use the ratio of number of hybrids to number of total cars sold in 2012 on one side of the proportion. Use the ratio of number of hybrids sold to x on the other side of the proportion.

Glossary

bargaining—coming to an agreement in which one person gives something in exchange for something else

budget—a plan for how money will be spent during a particular period or for a particular purchase

cargo—a load of items that is hauled from one place to another

chrome—a type of metal that is used to cover other metals in order to make them shiny

emit—to produce or release

equivalent ratios—two ratios that have the same value when simplified

fuel efficiency—the measure of how well a car uses fuel to travel certain distances

global positioning system (GPS)—a navigation system that allows people to determine their exact location

innovations—things that are new or different

maintenance—the work that is done to keep a machine or piece of equipment in good condition

negotiating—attempting to come to an agreement on something through discussion

percent—a part of a whole expressed in hundredths

proportion—an equation showing two equivalent ratios

rate—a ratio comparing an amount or distance to a period of time

ratio—a comparison of two quantities

standard—always supplied

statistics—a collection of numerical data

warranty—a guarantee on a purchased good that it is of good quality and will be replaced or repaired if something is wrong

Index

Let's Explore Math

Page 7:

a. 3:2; 5:6; 5:4

b. 185 cars

c. 15:37; 37:10

d. No; They are reciprocals.

e. It is important to express a ratio in words so that you know what each term in the ratio refers to.

Page 11:

a. 5:8; 8:5; 5:13; 8:13

b. Students should write a proportion like $\frac{5}{8} = \frac{n}{160}$; 100 white cars

c. Students should write a proportion like $\frac{8}{13} = \frac{n}{195}$; 120 black cars

d. 75 white cars; You could subtract 120 from 195 or solve a proportion like $\frac{5}{13} = \frac{n}{195}$.

Page 13:

a. $\frac{2}{15} = \frac{n}{90}$; 12 blue cars

b. $\frac{2}{15} = \frac{14}{n}$; 105 total cars

Page 21:

a. 720 miles per day

b. 8 mph

Page 23:

a. $\frac{150}{n} = \frac{80}{100}$; The original price was $187.50.

b. $\frac{45}{200} = \frac{n}{100}$; The discount was 22.5%.

Page 25:

a. Students should write a proportion like $\frac{20}{10} = \frac{x}{17}$; $34

b. Students should write a proportion like $\frac{8}{9} = \frac{x}{630}$; $560

c. Students should write a proportion like $\frac{2}{3} = \frac{250}{x}$; 375 cars

Problem-Solving Activity

a. 45:434; 78:377

b. 10%; 21%

c. Sports cars had the lowest average percentage of sales for the two years, so Mrs. Lee might want to decrease her sports car inventory.

d. A total of 812 cars would be sold in 2013.